the secrets
of the GREAT
COMMUNICATORS

the secrets of the GREAT COMMUNICATORS

PETER THOMPSON

an
ABC
BOOK

Published by ABC Enterprises for the
AUSTRALIAN BROADCASTING CORPORATION
GPO Box 9994 Sydney NSW 2001

National Library of Australia
Cataloguing-in-Publication entry
Thompson, Peter, 1952– .
  The secrets of the great communicators:

  ISBN 0 7333 0071 5.

  1. Orators. 2. Oratory. 3. Celebrities. I. Australian Broadcasting
  Corporation. II. Title.

808.5

Designed by Howard Binns-McDonald
Cover illustration by Geoff Morrison
Set in 10/11 pt Plantin by Caxtons Pty Ltd, South Australia
Printed and bound in Australia by Southwood Press, New South Wales
4-1295

*I dedicate this project to
my partner and wife, Lissa Tarleton.*

CONTENTS

INTRODUCTION _____ 9

PART ONE
THEIR FINEST HOUR _____ 11
Building Bridges _____ 12
Nerves _____ 13
Winston Churchill _____ 15
Communication and Technology _____ 17
Language and Gender _____ 18
Short Words—Short Speeches _____ 19
Pain and Reward _____ 20
Metaphor _____ 20
What You Can Do _____ 22

PART TWO
DREAMERS AND BELIEVERS _____ 25
Nazi Propaganda _____ 26
Mahatma Gandhi _____ 27
Mobilising Emotional Commitment _____ 28
The Greens Mobilise Emotional Energy _____ 29
Margaret Thatcher _____ 32
Black Dreamers and Believers _____ 33
What You Can Do _____ 36

PART THREE
JESUS SPOKE IN PARABLES _____ 37
Advertising as Story Telling _____ 38
The Stories of Great Events _____ 38
Actors as Story Tellers _____ 39
Ronald Reagan _____ 40
Humour _____ 47
Summary _____ 47
What You Can Do _____ 48

PART FOUR

THE CALL TO ACTION 49
Communication in Business 52
'Narrowcasting' 54
Bob Hawke 55
Conclusion 58
What You Can Do 60
Epilogue 61
Acknowledgments 63

INTRODUCTION

Discovering the secrets of the great communicators has great practical value. By analysing the communication techniques of famous people, we can better appreciate how they achieved their place in history and enhance our own skills.

Communication skills are not innate, just as reading and writing skills are not innate to children. Yet Australian education and training has undervalued the development of oral communication powers. Most adults suffer the consequences. A remarkable number of Australian professionals have communication skills well below their general level of professional skills. However, on occasions, most professionals will be judged by their ability to express themselves publicly.

There is perhaps no surer way of realising our potential as human beings than by developing self-expression. It is the means of being effective, influential, authoritative, even powerful. It is the rite of passage from being a passive to becoming an active participant in society. Great communicators develop their ability to say profound things simply, not simplistically. They listen as well as speak. They talk with emotion as well as reason.

This small book is not a step by step guide to public speaking or effective communication skills, although it does contain much practical advice. Its mission is to analyse how some great communicators came to be that way. The people analysed in particular detail—Churchill, Reagan, Thatcher and Hawke—are not all great communicators. I argue that Margaret Thatcher fails as a communicator because she is aloof and detached from her audience, and her style is manufactured; Bob Hawke, although once a great communicator, became vapid and repressed during his term of office as Prime Minister.

This book should be read in tandem with listening to the radio series and viewing the video, *The Secrets of the Great Communicators*. The chapter headings are the same as the titles of the four parts of the radio series. Much of the content of the book is the same as the radio and video scripts, the sound excerpts and interviews. However, in some places, the scripts are expanded to take in additional points and each chapter is concluded with a section on what you can do to adapt some of the techniques to your own presentations.

PART ONE

THEIR FINEST HOUR

The techniques of the great communicators can be learned and adapted—just as they learned and adapted them.

Australians are taught very little about communication. Although we have all spent a large slice of our lives as students, most of us have never spent a day learning the techniques of persuasive communication. As a result, most executives have communication skills far below their general level of professional skills.

Yet, communication skills are indispensable to management. In his landmark studies on what managers do, Henry Mintzberg, a professor at McGill University in Canada, said that managerial work is divided into three roles. First, '**interpersonal roles**' in which the manager acts as a figurehead, as a leader and a liaison-person. All this work requires communication skills. Then, the manager works in '**informational roles**', as a nerve centre, a disseminator of ideas and directions and a spokesman or spokeswoman. Again, all this work requires communication skills. And, finally, Henry Mintzberg says the manager works in '**decisional roles**', as an entrepreneur, a disturbance handler, a resource allocator and a negotiator. As you can see, managerial work is communications work—it involves a combination of public and interpersonal communication.

Great public communicators do a few things well. First, they build bridges to their audience. Finding common ground can disarm even a hostile audience. Second, a great speaker's feelings of conviction are the dominant message. Their feelings are never cool. Third, and of least importance, is the content of the message. It is least significant because audiences often forget *what* is said but they can always recall *how* it was said.

What is communication? According to my dictionary, the verb 'commune' means 'to have an intimate discussion with a friend or one's heart; together'. It comes from the middle English or old French *comuner* meaning to share.

Great communicators are people with outstanding ability to get their message across. And just as infants learn to talk, some adults learn to be great communicators.

Such learning may bear greatest fruit late in life. Winston Churchill was sixty-five at the outbreak of the Second World War. Ronald Reagan was president for most of his seventies. Both men, outstanding political actors of their time, dedicated their lives to developing the skills of communication.

This would have come as no surprise to the Ancient Greeks. They understood the power of oratory, or rhetoric, and developed precise rules for it. Oratory is as old as persuasion, politics, the courts of law and philosophy.

Oratory began with Homer, according to a book on the subject called *The Brutus* written by Cicero, the great Roman. Cicero said that the purpose of oratory is to delight, to teach or inform, and to move. Aristotle, in *The Politics*, wrote that the power of speech is what differentiates the human species from other animals. Through speech, humans can indicate the difference between good and evil, between what is just and unjust. Demosthenes, who lived in the fourth century before Christ, is regarded as being among the first orators. He wrote speeches for litigants in court, entered politics and was the Churchill of his day. The Roman, Lucius Annaeus Seneca declared: 'an orator is a good man skilled in speaking'. The good Seneca's own ability to speak inflamed the jealousy of Caligula, and he narrowly averted execution.

BUILDING BRIDGES

Great communicators build bridges, or create common ground, with their audiences. In June 1963, John F Kennedy visited Berlin. The city was the front line for the Cold War and a few years earlier the first Germans had built the wall to divide the city and the world. Kennedy skilfully built a bridge to his audience by breaking into German: 'Today, in the world of freedom, the proudest boast is: *Ich bin ein Berliner*'.

Jimmy Carter was another effective 'bridge builder'. He was virtually unknown as a national figure in the USA one year before being elected president in 1976. In the early months of his campaign, a Jimmy Carter speech would begin something like:

I'm Jimmy Carter. I come from a small town in the south; I'm a farmer, a churchgoer and a family man. I live with my wife Rosalynn and my young daughter Amy. I served in the navy and I was a nuclear engineer. I was governor of Georgia.

In a few lines Carter had built a bridge with a large part of any audience—all 'small-towners', farmers, churchgoers, families and veterans. He had also built a bridge to those who wanted to see evidence of occupational and political status. Carter gave a variation of this introduction thousands of times.

NERVES

Mark Twain once wrote: 'Tomorrow night I appear for the first time before a Boston audience—four thousand critics'. Mark Twain was summing up how we all feel when we're about to speak.

All communicators feel nervous. Indeed, nervousness is welcome because it gives energy to a performance. Without nerves, our presentations would be flat and lifeless. And speaking to people is a performance. Performers don't overcome nerves through experience. Laurence Olivier could hardly bring himself to go on stage in his sixties because of nerves. The singer, Carly Simon was phobic about live performances and on one occasion haemorrhaged on stage with an anxiety attack. The former Lord Mayor of Brisbane, Sallyanne Atkinson, is another person who feels terrified about talking publicly. Like Churchill and Carly Simon, Sallyanne Atkinson stuttered as a child. She had this to say:

I was a very timid and shy child, terrified of situations and terrified of talking to people, and a very bad stutterer from when I was eight until a little after I was married, until I had my first baby. I don't quite know what that means, I stopped stuttering after that. I don't feel shy now; I feel shy on occasions. When I have to make a speech I feel terrified.

Perhaps no woman has had more reason to feel terrified about speaking than Dame Enid Lyons when she became the first woman elected to the House of Representatives in 1943:

My first speech, oh, absolutely shattered me. I'd been in parliament a little over a week. And Mr Menzies, who was the leader of our party, said well now is the time for your speech. A maiden speech is a tremendous affair for the speaker and very interesting for other people to see how the new ones are going to shape up, particularly the first woman. I was terribly conscious of the enormous burden of responsibility I was carrying.

I had about an hour and a half to prepare ... But I couldn't prepare a speech. I walked up and down. I couldn't sit. I couldn't stand still. Then when I went into the parliament, I could scarcely move my legs. They were really stiff, I was so nervous. And then when I stood to speak my lips were stiff. I just felt I'd choke and the first few words sounded to me very indistinct. In a moment or two—I'm one of those people who respond very quickly to atmosphere—I got into my stride and filled in my half hour to the tick.

Dame Enid Lyons—from her maiden speech:

Mr Speaker. ... On my shoulders rests a great weight of responsibility because this is the first occasion on which a woman has addressed this House. For that reason it's an occasion which, for every woman in the Commonwealth, marks, in some degree, a turning point in history. I know that many honourable members have viewed the advent of women to the legislative halls with something approaching alarm. They feared, I have no doubt, the somewhat too vigorous use of a new broom. I wish to reassure them. I hold very sound views on brooms and sweeping. Although I quite realise that a new broom is a very useful adjunct to the work of the housewife, I also know that it's undoubtedly very unpopular in the broom cupboard. And this particular new broom knows that she has a very great deal to learn from, well, I dare not say, this particular cupboard.

The conservation leader, Bob Brown, is another nervous performer. As a sixteen-year-old he was made captain at Blacktown Boys High in Sydney. His nervousness was so acute that he developed a speech impediment which is unusual at that age. On several occasions as captain, he was so nervous when speaking that his tongue failed altogether. In embarrassment he would sit down.

As presenter of ABC Radio's long-running morning current affairs program, 'AM', I also suffer from nerves. Adrenalin pumps through my system each morning as I prepare to go on air. Twenty years in broadcasting hasn't diminished the sensation. I also feel the same way when I speak publicly to audiences.

The secret is to get our nerves working for us rather than against us. Breathing exercises are the answer. They are discussed at the end of part one.

WINSTON CHURCHILL

Kennedy said of Churchill that during England's darkest days and even darker nights, he mobilised the English language and sent it into battle.

Churchill's mastery of language and oratory was his lifetime's work. After a most unpromising start as a student, Churchill joined the military and soon took to journalism, writing as a war correspondent from battlefields in Cuba, the Sudan and South Africa. But following in the family tradition, his ambition was always politics and the spoken word would become his weapon. He confessed that throughout his youth 'it was my only ambition to be master of the spoken word'.

Churchill suffered many early disasters as a speaker. On one occasion in the House of Commons, his memory completely failed him. He sat down and clasped his head into his hands. This failure led to a new method of speech-making. Churchill discarded talking off-the-cuff in favour of reading from a full text. This habit prompted Churchill's great friend FE Smith to say: 'Winston spent the best years of his life writing impromptu speeches'. He would often sit in the bath to write. Eight hours preparation was usual for a forty-minute speech. The final draft of a speech would be written to verse, and could be read in a cadence or rhythm like rolling thunder.

In his fine biography, *The Last Lion*, William Manchester illustrates one example of how Churchill's speech would appear in verse form as he read it. The speech was delivered at St James Palace.

> We cannot yet see how deliverance will come
>   or when it will come
> but nothing is more certain
>   than that every trace of Hitler's footsteps
> every stain of his infected
>   and corroding fingers
> will be sponged and purged
>   and, if need be, blasted
>   from the surface of the earth.

This was high rhetoric suitable at a time when national survival was at stake. Churchill mastered the use of poetic technique: 'every stain of his infected and corroding fingers', 'will be sponged and purged and, if need be, blasted from the surface of the earth'.

Perhaps more than any statesman or stateswoman of the

century, Churchill's language continues to resonate in our ears. In his first speech to the House of Commons as prime minister on 13 May 1940, he summed up his position: 'I have nothing to offer but blood, toil, tears and sweat'. In that speech he mobilised every rhetorical device. The rhetorical question:

> You ask what is our policy? I will say it is to wage war by sea, land and air, with all our might and with all the strength that God can give us. To wage war against a monstrous tyranny, never surpassed in the dark and lamentable catalogue of human crime. That is our policy.

Then the rhetorical question followed by the skilful use of repetition to drive home the point:

> You ask what is our aim? I can answer in one word—victory. Victory at all costs. Victory in spite of all terror. Victory, however long and hard the road may be. For without victory there is not survival.

After the evacuation from Dunkirk, the Battle of Britain began. On 4 June 1940, Churchill again addressed the House. Again, he worked with repetition:

> We shall fight in France. We shall fight on the seas and oceans. We shall fight with growing confidence and growing strength in the air. We shall defend our island, whatever the cost may be. We shall fight on the beaches. We shall fight on the landing grounds. We shall fight in the fields and in the streets. We shall fight in the hills. We shall never surrender.

The wartime prime minister lived by a heavy schedule, sleeping little and working through much of the night in his underground headquarters. It seems his schedule was so busy that he elected to have a stand-in actor read many of his most famous speeches on the BBC. It's now believed that soon after taking over the role as prime minister, Churchill would read a speech in the House of Commons, and then the actor Norman Shelley would re-read it on the BBC sometime later. Thus, many of Churchill's most famous speeches, including the one above, 'We shall fight on the beaches ...', were read by Norman 'Winston Churchill' Shelley. Churchill himself did not record the speeches until he signed up with a recording company to make a set of his wartime speeches in the 1950s.

Churchill was passionate about how language sounded. William Manchester wrote, in *The Last Lion*, that 'Churchill's feeling for the English tongue was sensual, almost erotic; when he coined a phrase he would suck it, rolling it around his palate to extract its full flavour'. On one occasion Lloyd George complained to Churchill that he should not use such ripe language in attacking the Italian duce Mussolini's actions in Ethiopia. Churchill replied, 'Ah, the b's in those words: 'obsolete', 'reprehensible'. You must pay attention to euphony'. By euphony, Churchill was referring, of course, to how language sounded.

Churchill employed his long periods in the political wilderness to develop his interest in writing and language. He wrote a history of World War I—*The World Crisis*, a six volume history of World War II, and *A History of the English Speaking Peoples*. In 1953, he was awarded the Nobel prize for literature. The citation referred to Churchill's mastery in historical and biographical presentation and his brilliant oratory.

COMMUNICATION AND TECHNOLOGY

Even by 1940s' standards, Churchill was an old-fashioned communicator and it may have required the gravity of war for his ponderous and oratorical style to work on that most intimate of forums—the radio.

In our century, communicators have adapted to successive revolutions in technology. Radio and television, which put the communicator's message directly into the people's homes, have led to the decline in importance of the platform speech. In its place, there has been the growing need for communicators to develop the question and answer skills of a conversation or interview.

When Theodore Roosevelt became president of the United States in the first year of this century, sound recording and the public address system were new phenomena. Theodore Roosevelt's distant cousin, Franklin Roosevelt, who entered the White House in 1933, was the first president to use the new medium, radio. In the twelve years of his presidency he presented twenty-seven so called 'fireside chats', an average of one every five months. They weren't chats in the style we'd imagine. They lacked intimacy and sounded more like platform speeches.

Post-war, the technology changed again. John F Kennedy became the television president. The 1960 campaign for the White House was regarded as lacklustre until, for the first time, the candidates debated on television. In a demonstration of the primacy of the medium over the message, there was widespread discussion, after the first of four debates, on the effect of a five o'clock shadow on the face of Kennedy's opponent, Richard Nixon. To some eyes, the shadow made Nixon look shifty. Kennedy's winning margin was a little more than 100 000 votes and, in all probability, Kennedy's strong performance in the television debates was the deciding factor. Although the debates are now an integral feature of presidential elections, the second round of debates was not held until Gerald Ford and Jimmy Carter met in 1976.

Communicating on radio and television required quite different skills than those needed for talking from the platform and soap box. The oratory of the set speech didn't fit in the intimacy of people's homes. More than ever—plain, simple, short words and down-to-earth language became the language of the effective communicator. The 'calm' voice replaced the 'raised' voice, which was now a threatening voice.

Radio and television are so called mass media, but people listen and watch either alone or in small groups. The effective radio or television message has to be personalised.

LANGUAGE AND GENDER

Whatever the medium of delivery, language remains the building block of communication. It defines meaning and relationships of power.

The Australian academic, Dale Spender, has strong views on how the gender orientation of language places women in a subordinate role to men:

Men have been in a position to make up the words and the way the words are used. They have done so very much to their own advantage. I would like to see women also having access to making up some of the words and some of the conditions for their use, and I would like to see both co-exist. I don't want to replace one with the other but at the moment men have a monopoly on meaning. What that means is that problems that men encounter in their lives are very well encoded. There are lots of synonyms, lots of words to describe them. But problems that are unique to women, there are simply no words to describe them. And there are also few opportunities for them to talk about the fact that there are no words.

Language forms our image of the world. And professional language users, such as politicians and community leaders, teachers, lawyers and judges, journalists and broadcasters, bear particular responsibility for ensuring that language is not used to stereotype people by sex and race. I recently held an animated discussion with a judge about his reluctance to find a replacement word for 'foreman' of the jury. We agreed that 'foreperson' sounds awkward and absurd. However, even alternative words such as jury 'leader' or 'chair' or 'facilitator' are preferable to 'foreman' because they break the nexus between a position of authority and gender.

SHORT WORDS – SHORT SPEECHES

Churchill made the case for simplicity with eloquence when he said: 'I like short words'.

The American historian Barbara Tuchman said the same: short words are always preferable to long ones. Barbara Tuchman knew how to express herself. Her splendid books, *August 1914*, *The Proud Tower* and *The March of Folly*, to name a few, are among the most readable books of history. Barbara Tuchman wrote about her craft in the book, *Practising History*. She liked the monosyllables, beautiful and pure, like 'bread', 'sun' and 'grass'.

Barbara Tuchman pointed to these wonderful words by the American writer Ralph Waldo Emerson as the purest form of writing. They are about the beginnings of the American War of Independence at Concord, Massachusetts.

By the rude bridge that arched the flood
Their flag to April's breeze unfurled,
Here once the embattled farmers stood,
And fired the shot heard round the world.

There are twenty-eight words; twenty-four of them are monosyllables.

Abraham Lincoln's most famous speech, the Gettysburg address, is another example of economy in language. It contained only two hundred and sixty-eight words. Another president, Franklin D Roosevelt, advised that when making speeches: 'Be sincere, be brief, be seated'.

Speakers and writers who purge their communications of clutter are giving their audience a gift. Tuchman recalled the letter written by the scientist and theologian Pascal: 'I am sorry to have wearied you with so long a letter but I did not have time to write you a short one'.

The television era has conditioned us into having very short attention spans. In this age of 'busy-ness' we can quickly exhaust the patience of our audience. Yet speakers rarely resist the temptation to talk too long. I am astonished at how many speakers drone on, apparently unconcerned by the drowsiness of their audience.

However, talking quickly is not the solution. The most comfortable speed for both delivering and receiving information is *adagio*, which means 'at ease'. When we talk at ease our voice falls to its lower registers and we increase the natural authority of our speech.

PAIN AND REWARD

I mentioned earlier that Churchill would spend about eight hours writing a forty-minute speech. When I told this fact to the head of Celebrity Speakers in Sydney, Christine Maher, she seemed surprised—not by how much time it took but by how little. Preparing a great presentation takes great time.

A speaker has much in common with a soloist in the concert hall. The music appears to flow spontaneously yet the performance is fully rehearsed. The American economist, John Kenneth Galbraith departed from his Harvard ivory tower and wrote books and gave speeches which everyone could understand. He confessed: 'There are days when the result is so bad that no fewer than five revisions are required. In contrast, when I'm greatly inspired, only four revisions are needed'.

METAPHOR

Great communicators develop great metaphors. A metaphor is a figure of speech in which one object is likened to another as if it were that other, as 'He was a lion in battle'. It is distinguished from a simile by the fact that a metaphor does not employ any words of comparison such as 'like' or 'as'. Metaphors define relationships between things. They can create relationships where they didn't previously exist. Metaphors are perhaps the most powerful tools of language.

Sometimes metaphors enter history, such as Churchill's 'blood, toil, tears and sweat'. Paul Keating sent financial markets into panic when he said, on commercial radio in 1986, that Australia could become a 'banana republic'. Bill Hayden, when he was dumped from the Labor leadership on the eve of the 1983 election, said, metaphorically, that a drover's dog could have led the party to victory the way the country was and the way the opinion polls were showing up. Few memorable metaphors just slip off the tongue. Paul Keating is reputed to try out many of his famous remarks well before they are aired publicly. Rehearsal ensures that when the moment comes for their delivery, the timing will be right.

Metaphors create powerful visual imagery and can condense an argument into a few words. When the conservation leader Bob Brown was asked during the campaign to save Tasmania's Franklin River: 'Wouldn't flooding the Franklin destroy only a small part of the wilderness?', he replied, 'Flooding the Franklin would be like putting a scratch across the Mona Lisa or a Beethoven record'. In a few words he had captured the essence of the argument. Claude Levi-Strauss, the French social anthropologist, wrote that 'metaphor, far from being a decoration that is added to language, purifies it and restores it to its original nature'.

Martin Luther King was perhaps the finest orator of this century. His historic speech, 'I have a dream', which was delivered in 1963 on the steps of the Lincoln Memorial in Washington before more than two hundred thousand people, drew much of its power from metaphor:

Five score years ago, a great American in whose symbolic shadow we stand today signed the emancipation proclamation. This momentous decree came as a great beacon light of hope to millions of negro slaves who had been seared in the flames of withering injustice. It came as a joyous daybreak to end the long night of their captivity.

But one hundred years later the negro is still not free. One hundred years later the life of the negro is still sadly crippled by the manacles of segregation and the chains of discrimination. One hundred years later the negro lives on a lonely island of poverty in the midst of a vast ocean of material prosperity. One hundred years later, the negro is still languishing in the corners of American society and finds himself an exile in his own land. So we have come here today to dramatise a shameful condition.

In a sense we have come to our nation's capital to cash a cheque. When the architects of our republic wrote the magnificent words of the Constitution and the Declaration of

Independence, they were signing a promissory note to which every American was to fall heir. This note was a promise that all men, yes black men as well as white men, would be guaranteed the unalienable rights of life, liberty and the pursuit of happiness.

It is obvious today that America has defaulted on this promissory note insofar as her citizens of colour are concerned. Instead of honouring this sacred obligation, America has given the negro people a bad cheque; a cheque which has come back marked 'insufficient funds'.

I will discuss Martin Luther King's speech in further detail in Part Two.

WHAT YOU CAN DO

Most human behaviour is learned through modelling others. Of course, children's games often model the adult world. Modelling is also an effective way of learning communication skills. People who are keen to improve their communication should seek out model presenters and speakers. We can also learn a great deal by critically analysing the way information is presented to us. By recognising our own positive responses, we can use the same techniques when it's our turn to stand and deliver.

Be aware that nerves are an integral part of performance and that you can get them to work for you rather than against you by practising breathing and speech exercises.

Breathing exercises work for a very physiological reason. When we are tense and fearful, our diaphragm rises and contracts the available space in our lungs. We become short of breath. If we talk when we are breathless we sometimes squeak. Yoga teachers know that by controlling our breathing we begin to relax. Before you begin a presentation take long, deep breaths. Try to fill your lungs as though you're breathing from your lower back. One technique worth trying is: first breathe out, pause for five seconds, now allow your lungs to fill with air. As your lungs expand you can feel your body relax. No professional performer merely steps on stage. Singers don't sing, actors don't act, broadcasters shouldn't broadcast, speakers shouldn't speak, without a warm-up which involves breathing exercises to deal with nerves.

Speech exercises are equally important. The vocal chords need opening. By sounding the alphabet: 'a,a,a,a,; b,b,b,b,' we get the tongue moving. It's like an athlete's warm-up for the tongue. Try some particularly difficult phrases like 'red leather, yellow leather' or 'Colin's cousins cover canary cages with cloth'. To clear and open your throat, say 'ah-ah-ah' as you would to a doctor examining your tonsils.

Work to develop the ability to use metaphor to cut to the essence of what you're saying. Build bridges to your audience based on common points of identity. Recognise that everyone has the power to become an effective communicator. Like Churchill, we can make it our 'ambition to be master of the spoken word'. There is no more empowering investment of our time.

PART TWO

DREAMERS AND BELIEVERS

In June 1968, in one of those most painful episodes of recent history, America buried another Kennedy. Robert F Kennedy had just won the California primary election for the Democrats and now looked assured of the party's nomination to contest the presidency in November against the Republican candidate Richard Nixon. Bobby Kennedy died before developing his full potential. David Halberstam, author of *The Best and the Brightest* and *The Unfinished Odyssey of Robert Kennedy*, thought he might have made another Lincoln. At Bobby Kennedy's funeral, his brother Edward delivered the eulogy. Borrowing words from George Bernard Shaw, he said, 'Some people see things as they are and say why. I dream things that never were and ask why not?'

What separates the dreamers and believers from their followers? The dreamers and believers—through speech and language—create our image of the world. Through their mastery of language, they capture our hearts. In *The Prince* Machiavelli wrote that:

> Men nearly always follow the tracks made by others and proceed in their affairs by imitation, even though they cannot entirely keep to the tracks of others or emulate the prowess of their models. So a prudent man should always follow in the footsteps of great men and imitate those who have been outstanding.

Some among the 'princes' or dreamers leave an indelible mark. They are passionate people and many of them are among the great communicators. When people feel strongly and say what they feel rather than just what they think, they have the raw material for great communication.

In another context, George Bernard Shaw also wrote that 'the reasonable man adapts himself to the world; the unreasonable one persists in trying to adapt the world to himself. Therefore all progress depends on the unreasonable man'. The dreamers and believers are often unreasonable men and women who feel strongly about the world and talk from the heart in order to change it. By listening to them we realise that passion is central to persuasion.

Many of us fear the potency of passion. Indeed, the more formal education we have, the more likely we are to reject an argument based on instinct and feeling. Too often, we cling to sober rationality as the only means we permit ourselves for persuading others. Many lawyers and academics are professional rationalists who deliberately purge their language of feeling and subjectivity. But as a consequence they mostly fail to be great communicators.

NAZI PROPAGANDA

Our fear of unleashed passion is understandable. Wrongly directed, its impact can be diabolical. The Nazi leaders of the Third Reich were master manipulators of mass emotion. They turned propaganda into 'art'. The most careful attention was paid to the creation of pageantry. Only Hitler himself could approve the design drawings for a major rally.

A sense of the theatre of Nazi rallies is conveyed by the Swedish film director Ingmar Bergman. In his autobiography *The Magic Lantern* he recalls being present, as a youth, at a pre-war Nazi rally in Germany. Bergman says he had never seen such an eruption of energy. He shouted, held out his arm, howled and loved it 'like everyone else'.

The decorations for Hitler's rallies were often designed by Hitler's chief architect and later armaments minister, Albert Speer. In his book *Inside the Third Reich*, Albert Speer described his own seduction this way:

> Hitler's magnetic force, his persuasiveness, the peculiar magic of his by no means pleasant voice, the oddity of his rather banal manner, the seductive simplicity with which he attacked the complexity of our problems—all that bewildered and fascinated. The mood he cast was much deeper than the speech itself, most of which I didn't remember for long. He had taken hold of me before I had grasped what was happening.

Although documentaries often portray Hitler as a raving fanatic, such techniques made up only a small part of his speaking style. Speer says that everything about Hitler's style bore out the note of reasonable modesty. He would begin his speeches in a low voice, somewhat shyly and hesitantly. It was more an historical lecture than a speech. Soon his pitch would rise and he would speak urgently and with hypnotic persuasiveness. Speer says:

> Finally, Hitler no longer seemed to be speaking to convince; rather he seemed to feel that he was expressing what the audience, by now transformed into a single mass, expected of him.

What are we to make of Hitler's oratorical style now? I consulted Hugh Mackay, a communications specialist and the head of Mackay Research in Sydney:

> What Hitler did, and the words are borrowed from Carl Jung, was to magnify the inaudible whisper in the German soul. That's a rather poetic way of saying that he released feelings which were strong in the German people. It's not what Hitler did to the Germans. It's what the Germans were already thinking and feeling which Hitler, in a sense, gave them permission to think and feel. He became almost a receptacle for the views, the prejudices, the outrage, the anxieties, the insecurities, the aspirations of the German people. He was their focus.

MAHATMA GANDHI

Half a world away from Hitler's Germany lived a man with a wholly different moral purpose. Mohandas 'Mahatma' Gandhi had no official voice and held no positions of power, but led a nation. In his memoir on Gandhi, William Shirer wrote:

> Gandhi was not an orator. He scarcely raised his voice and made no gestures. I doubt if the vast majority in the huge crowds ever caught his words. They were fulfilled by the sight of him, and especially by receiving his *darshan* or blessing.

Gandhi's communication technique was leading by example, not words. He practised what Saint Francis of Assisi said—'It's no use walking anywhere to preach unless our walking is our preaching'.

Gandhi may have been no orator but he was a great communicator. He mobilised the emotional energy of Indians by his brazen but non-violent defiance. He understood the power of symbols. He discarded his western suits for the traditional loincloth worn by the masses. Churchill was revolted that a British trained lawyer, posing as a fakir, would stride half-naked up the steps of the vice-regal palace to parley on equal terms with the representative of the king-emperor. Yet Gandhi in his loincloth was communicating a powerful message. He was mobilising the emotional commitment of the Indian masses.

MOBILISING EMOTIONAL COMMITMENT

Whatever sort of audience you may find yourself addressing—people at a public meeting, your clients, or even the board of directors—you must mobilise emotional commitment.

Decisions and actions are rarely taken on a rational basis alone. And, if they are, people won't feel committed to them. Throughout history, great social movements, great businesses and great ideas have all depended for their success on emotional energy. Great communicators always energise people emotionally.

The experts on communication agree. Christine Maher is the founder of the agency Celebrity Speakers in Sydney. She also has long experience in training people to become effective communicators. She says the Greeks understood the role of emotion in persuasion and speech-making two and a half thousand years ago.

> They thought there were three components in a speech. One was called the *ethos* and that was the credibility of the person speaking and I would equate that with who's talking and why should I listen to them. They also said that the *logos* was important; we still have the word in our language, that is, 'the words'. But they placed great emphasis on what they called *pathos* and that was the whole person being involved with what they were saying. Any good speech involves making contact, not only intellectually, not only through the ears, but also through the heart or the guts.

Another consultant in communications, Dr Peter Kenny, worked for many years with the advertising whiz John Singleton. He is also a former head of research at the ABC and I asked him about the key to effective communication.

> KENNY: It has to be emotional. You have to, first of all, set up an emotional field or tone of some kind and I usually express that as going to the cliff edge. You've got to arouse people. The only necessary condition for good persuasive communication is

that you arouse people, by whatever means you can.

THOMPSON: And what are those means?

KENNY: Well, all the way from irritation, anger, resentment and conflict on one end, down to the nice emotions like sentimentality, patriotism, goosebumps; the sort of things which happen in soap opera. Any kind of emotion will do.

Hugh Mackay of Mackay Research:

I don't think taking the audience to the edge is quite enough, it's not the whole story. Of course it is essential that emotional arousal occurs but it has to be emotional arousal that is focused on something that is significant, relevant, and interesting to the audience. We have to remember that what's in the audience determines the outcome of a communication encounter. Now of course, emotion is in the audience and that's what has to be unlocked or released, but it also has to be focused. It's what the audience does with the message that determines the outcome, not what the message does to the audience. I think we have to remember the pre-eminence of the audience in this whole process.

THE GREENS MOBILISE EMOTIONAL ENERGY

Perhaps no social movement in recent Australian history has so successfully mobilised emotional energy as the conservationists. If Hugh Mackay is correct in saying that the audience is pre-eminent in the process of communication, then Australian audiences have been ready to hear messages about protecting the environment. Social surveys now rank concern for the environment as the most important issue for Australians after the economy. Some surveys report that it's the number one priority.

Critics of the green movement typify it as being led by fanatics who are spearheading an emotional wave of popular sentiment bordering on the hysterical. The critics are right in recognising the role of emotion or feeling in generating the energy which has propelled the environmentalists into becoming a powerful political force. The greens have been great populist communicators.

The Australian green movement has been lent powerful support by world celebrities such as David Bellamy, David Attenborough and David Suzuki. The three Davids made their names as television presenters, but each has scientific credentials. Their populist styles of presentation have made ecological issues come alive for millions of people.

Each of the Davids has a markedly different approach. On location, David Bellamy swings through the trees or pops out from behind broad-leafed plants, inviting us by his words and by his ample gesturing to feel as excited as he is. Bellamy is right at home in the wilderness. David Attenborough has a more avuncular, Sherlock Holmes style forensic approach. His warm voice envelops us as we peer into the natural mysteries with him. David Suzuki's appeal is verbal. He addresses us on radio or television or in a public hall. He skilfully balances emotion and reason. Engaging as Davids Bellamy, Attenborough and Suzuki are, they are only a sideshow in the Australian conservation movement's communications effort.

Jonathan West is a former director of the Wilderness Society and a former adviser to Barry Cohen when he was minister for the environment in the Hawke government. Jonathan says the greens are specialists in talking in visual images.

The great strength of the green movement, particularly the nature conservation movement, has been in images, not in technical arguments. Successful environmental advocates have always been able to create word pictures. It's more spiritual type arguments, you might say emotional arguments, that have been successful in generating support. The technical arguments have been necessary to rebut the other side's point of view but haven't been the heart of the message from the environmentalists.

Consultant Peter Kenny says:

The environmental movement understands what I'm talking about: that you have to do showbiz. It's no good just putting a rational argument in a cool way. You have to go out in public and put on some kind of show—tie yourself to a tree, bury yourself in the ground, get up a telegraph pole. That's good showbiz, so it's going to get on televison; we're going to watch it; it's going to get to us. Whereas the environmentalists understand that, the people who are trying to oppose them don't understand it. I've had talks with the Coal Tribunal, for example, where they couldn't get their minds around the fact that they had to go to the cliff edge and do showbiz and arouse emotion in order to put their arguments that were contrary to the environmentalists.

For more than a decade, Dr Bob Brown has been the leading

figure in the Australian conservation movement. In part one I mentioned how Bob Brown was intensely nervous when he was required to speak as school captain at Blacktown Boys High in Sydney. I met Bob Brown in 1972 and have followed his involvement in public issues from the beginning. He was then, and remains, a nervous speaker. When he is tired, which is often, he can be a poor public speaker. He is rarely smooth in delivery. He reads aloud badly. But, when he is talking emotionally about the wilderness and nature, he is rivetting. Bob Brown is a great communicator when he leaves behind the world of arid facts and talks from the heart about an approaching storm or an autumn haze or the crystal light of a snow flake or the wash of pure water on the bank of a wild river. Bob Brown is a dreamer and believer in the great tradition of activists for social change. Talking about Brown, Jonathan West says:

> Bob is able to communicate his own simple warmth and honesty through his manner, through the tone of his voice, through the words that he uses. Everyone who meets him sees that he is the same guy on the media as he is in person. The other great talent that Bob has is to create these word pictures. For example, when someone says 'we're just putting a little road through a wilderness area', he's able to create a picture by saying 'that's like putting a scratch across the face of the Mona Lisa. The vast majority of the Mona Lisa is intact but the scratch spoils it'. The long, detailed, technical explanation about the way in which the road would reduce the amount of wilderness square kilometres would have nothing like the same impact as a simple word image like that.

I asked Bob Brown this question: 'What are the keys to successful communication?'

> Communicating with people is being able to relate to them as if they were neighbours or friends. To treat them as human beings you've known for a long time—who recognise that you are a human being also. To be able to cut across what's often a complicated message in simple form. To put it across as if you mean it because you do have to mean it if you are going to communicate. And to remember that they are intelligent people who are going to make up their minds, given the information, the same as you can yourself.

I also posed the following question to Bob Brown: 'When you talk, you talk very emotionally, don't you?'

> Emotions are really important. We are emotional beings. Our whole relationship with the planet is based on millions of

years of a developing emotional relationship. We come from the wilderness. We were cradled by it and we have a bond with nature which we must be able to express if we are going to save this planet.

MARGARET THATCHER

When I referred earlier to George Bernard Shaw's dictum that it's the unreasonable men and women who change the world, few better fit the description than Margaret Thatcher. Her uncompromising determination to steer Britain towards a new path defied the modern image of political leaders as merely reactive to opinion polls and popular sentiment. But Margaret Thatcher isn't a great communicator. Although she projected strength and determination, she never really dared to run on feelings, to be emotional. Part of Margaret Thatcher remains detached.

Shortly before Margaret Thatcher retired, I consulted Hugo Young, a commentator in Britain's *Guardian* newspaper and the author of *One of Us*, a biography marking ten years of Mrs Thatcher's rule. He commented:

I think there are very few things which she's ever said which will be remembered. For somebody who's been in power for such an incredibly long time the number of phrases which are associated with her, the number of speeches she's made which people remember are extraordinarily few. And the phrases with which she's associated are almost always written by her speechwriters. She's not a great extemporary speaker, she's a poor parliamentary speaker, she's a very considerable fighting speaker but she's not a great orator.

One of the truths about British prime ministers these days is that they almost never make speeches to audiences which are not already converted. All the security considerations require that when they are out in the country they speak to invited audiences who are, by definition, members of the party. And in the House of Commons, because she's always had a large majority behind her, she's never had the job of persuading people.

She's not like Churchill, she's not even like Macmillan, she's not even like Ted Heath, all of whom had at various moments of their careers—Churchill most conspicuously— great moments of rhetorical power. She's had almost none.

I think she's always been aware of the tremendous importance of communication while never being very good at it. She employed a lot of assistance in trying to convey her message by television and in manicuring, most carefully, the party political broadcasts which she's made. She would like to be able to speak directly to the people in a way which is persuasive. She's never been able to do this because, I think, it goes back to the fact that she's never been very popular, people haven't liked her very much. In her manner, she's always speaking down to people; it is manifestly insincere and manufactured and doesn't really come from the heart.

As Hugo Young says—despite her limitations at the art, Mrs Thatcher understood the importance of communication. And she worked to develop the skills. She employed a speech tutor at the National Theatre and began a program of humming exercises to lower the pitch or timbre of her voice. The theory is that a lower voice increases the tone of authority. In the book *Our Master's Voices*, the British academic Max Atkinson claims that Mrs Thatcher lowered the pitch of her voice by forty-six hertz—half the difference between the average male and female voice. What's more, she achieved this feat at an age when the average woman's voice is rising in pitch.

I asked the Australian communications specialist Christine Maher whether Margaret Thatcher succeeds as a communicator.

I think she does not. I think she is perceived by people to be too much of a created communicator. She's certainly improved over the years but she lacks the apparent ease and spontaneity, if you like, of Reagan. She has somehow been manufactured.

In Part Three we see how Margaret Thatcher admired the communication skills of her friend and ally across the Atlantic—Ronald Reagan.

BLACK DREAMERS AND BELIEVERS

In this century the burden of dreaming for a greater world has fallen disproportionately on the shoulders of black leaders. In South Africa, Nelson Mandela and Steve Biko have communicated with the disenfranchised black majority through their words and unimpeachable personal behaviour and sacrifice. After twenty-seven years of being silenced by imprisonment Nelson Mandela emerged with a dignified, coherent and lucid message of hope. Archbishop Desmond Tutu, as the humanitarian and liberal voice of black Africa, appealed to an international audience for support in wearing down the walls of apartheid. In 1984 the archbishop was awarded the Nobel Peace Prize. In the United States, Jesse Jackson is the voice of black America. Few public figures are so daringly emotional—as he demonstrated in the 1984 and 1988 presidential campaigns.

Barbara Jordan, a black former member of congress who is also an outstanding speaker, had this to say about Jesse Jackson:

> Jesse Jackson has been successful in getting some white people to vote for him. He has always been successful in getting large numbers of blacks to vote for him. It is good that white people can see a black person being articulate and exciting on the stump.

Jesse Jackson is, of course, heir to black America's most gifted speaker—perhaps the greatest speaker of this century—Martin Luther King.

Alexander Herzen, the 19th-century Russian philosopher, said that 'you can waken people by dreaming their dreams more clearly than they dream themselves'. Martin Luther King's dream entered history. His Washington speech in August 1963 came at the height of the non-violent campaign by black Americans to free themselves from a century of segregation. Martin Luther King wrote 'I have a dream' on the night before its delivery. He had used the theme, 'I have a dream', once before in Detroit. King's colleague, Ralph Abernathy, says the Holy Spirit took hold of Martin Luther King. Midway through his speech, King put aside his notes and emotion filled his eyes:

> I still have a dream. It is a dream deeply rooted in the American dream. I have a dream that one day, this nation will rise up and live out the true meaning of its creed—'we hold these truths to be self evident that all men are created equal'. I have a dream that one day on the red hills of Georgia, the sons of former slaves and the sons of former slave owners will be able to sit down at the table of brotherhood. I have a dream that one day, even the state of Mississippi, a state sweltering with the heat of injustice, sweltering with the heat of oppression, will be transformed into an oasis of freedom and justice. I have a dream that my four little children will one day live in a nation where they will not be judged by the colour of their skin but by the content of their character. I have a dream today.

I have a dream that one day, down in Alabama with its vicious racists, with its governor having his lips dripping with the words of interposition and nullification, one day right there in Alabama, little black boys and black girls will be able to join hands with little white boys and white girls as sisters and brothers. I have a dream today.

I have a dream that one day every valley shall be exalted, and every hill and mountain shall be made low, the rough places will be made plains, and the crooked places will be made straight, and the glory of the Lord shall be revealed, and all flesh shall see it together.

This is our hope. This is the faith I go back to the south with. With this faith we will be able to hew out of the mountain of despair a stone of hope. With this faith we will be able to transform the jangling discords of our nation into a beautiful symphony of brotherhood. With this faith we will be able to work together, to pray together, to struggle together, to go to gaol together, to stand up for freedom together, knowing that we will be free one day.

This will be the day when all of God's children will be able to sing with new meaning 'My country 'tis of thee, sweet land of liberty, of thee I sing. Land where my fathers died, land of the pilgrim's pride, from every mountainside let freedom ring'. And if America is to be a great nation this must become true.

Let freedom ring from the mighty mountains of New York. Let freedom ring from the heightening Alleghenies of Pennsylvania, let freedom ring from the snow topped Rockies of Colorado, let freedom ring from the curvaceous slopes of California. But not only that, let freedom ring from Stone Mountain of Georgia. Let freedom ring from Lookout Mountain of Tennessee. Let freedom ring from every hill and molehill of Mississippi. From every mountainside, let freedom ring.

When we allow freedom to ring, when we let it ring from every village and every hamlet, from every state and every city, we will be able to speed up that day when all of God's children, black men and white men, jews and gentiles, protestants and catholics, will be able to join hands and sing in the words of the old negro spiritual, 'Free at last, free at last, thank God almighty, we are free at last'.

The dreamers and believers have tapped the most important source of power in communication—emotion. Most of us fear expressing our feelings, particularly in public forums. But feelings connect people. Without them, a speech is dry and abstract. When people have the courage to say how they feel about those things they really care about, rather than just what they think, they have crossed the bridge to great communication. And if you combine feelings with a well-told story, people will remember what you say. That is the subject of Part Three.

WHAT YOU CAN DO

You can mobilise your own emotional energy by speaking on things about which you feel strongly. The surest way to capture feelings is to talk about events from your personal experience. These stories have the added virtue that you know them well, and so do not have to write extensive notes. In my own communication workshops I have been amazed by the responses when I ask people to talk about something they really care about. The least skilful communicators suddenly become empowered.

So, in preparing a presentation, search out relevant stories from your own experience which fit the topic. Do not be afraid to use the 'I' word. Audiences thirst for frankness and candour. Audiences want to share your dreams and beliefs, not abstractions.

Never give a presentation of facts which doesn't include how you feel about them. Next time you speak, be bold, go to the cliff edge and test the response.

PART THREE

JESUS SPOKE IN PARABLES

Jesus got his message across. He spoke in parables. In part three we consider how talking in stories helps make people remember what we say and is among the most powerful communication techniques.

In the first two sections, we explored the potential of language and metaphor to create images—remember Churchill's 'blood, toil, tears and sweat'. Then we considered how Martin Luther King released emotional energy in 'I have a dream'. Without emotions, speech and communication are dry and lifeless. Another way which helps people to really connect with us is to talk in stories—stories which simplify the point we want to make and which give substance to abstract ideas. Talking simply need never mean talking simplistically. The best stories are usually our own eyewitness accounts.

After two thousand years, we still remember the stories of a great preacher. Jesus used parables as his communication technique.

Hugh Mackay of Mackay Research:

I think Jesus Christ demonstrated through the parables that anecdotes are very powerful and it's still the case that some of the greatest communicators never, as it were, strip down what their policy statement is. They always express it anecdotally. They tell you a story which illustrates the point they want to make. And it's the value of soap operas on television. We more easily identify with events unfolding than we can with philosophical principles. And in our ordinary lives we gradually develop our philosophical position, say, in response to the un- folding of our own story. So I don't think it's surprising that parable, anecdote and story telling are really the most powerful form of communication, in the sense of the audience being most easily able to project itself right into the story.

ADVERTISING AS STORY TELLING

S tory telling has commercial as well as divine power. The adver-
tising guru David Ogilvy explained the story of the humble Hathaway shirt to Robert Moore on ABC's 'Monday Conference' in the 1970s.

OGILVY: I once had to do an advertising campaign for a brand of shirts. There's nothing remarkable about just showing a photograph of a man in a shirt; why should anybody look at it? So I put a patch on the man's eye and photographed him like that. And for some reason best known to God, it rescued me from obscurity, made me famous and made my client frightfully rich.

MOORE: Well, apart from God, do you have insight as to why it worked?

OGILVY: Well, I'll tell you this. There's a curious factor in advertising. If you inject into the photograph in an advertise-ment what we call 'story appeal', people's curiosity is roused. And maybe if you see a man in an ad with a patch on his eye then you'll wonder what's that about. Then you'll read the ad, then you'll go and buy the shirt.

THE STORIES OF GREAT EVENTS

M ost story telling involves relating past events. Describing
something which is happening 'live' requires special skills. Sometimes these stories, if they are of great events, become the stuff of our history, myth and legend.

In September 1940 the Luftwaffe was raining its terror on London. America stood outside the war, sympathetic to Britain but detached. In that pre-television age, Americans' image of the Battle of Britain was conveyed in words, on radio. The great American reporter Ed Murrow told the story as he watched the skies.

I'm standing on a rooftop looking out over London. At the moment everything is quiet. For reasons of national as well as personal security I'm unable to tell you the exact location from which I'm speaking. Off to my left, far away in the distance I can see just the faint red angry snap of an anti-aircraft burst against this steel blue sky. But the guns are so far away it's impossible to hear them from this location. Everything is quiet. More searchlights spring up over on my right. I think probably in a minute we shall have the sound of guns in the immediate vicinity. The lights are swinging over in this general direction now. You'll hear two explosions ... there they are. Again, moving in, still a considerable distance away. Moving still just a little closer. There you heard two. The searchlights are stretching out now in this general direction. I can hear just the faint whisper of an aircraft high overhead.

Broadcaster Richard Dimbleby was another gifted story teller, also witnessing a great event. It was November 1963, the funeral of John F Kennedy.

And so outside to the sunshine, where the bearer party, some of them coloured servicemen, drawn from all the services, proudly, reverently and carefully, bear their dead president and commander-in-chief down the steep steps, back to the gun carriage which waits for them at the bottom. Cardinal Cushing sprinkles holy water on the coffin and kisses it. Somewhere high above a single bell is tolling. The slow, careful party moves on to the gun carriage. Mrs Kennedy, the children, the other mourners follow down the steps behind. The presidential flag, the American eagle between the arrow of war and the dove of peace but facing the dove of peace, is borne away to take its place in the procession, for the journey to the national cemetery at Arlington.

ACTORS AS STORY TELLERS

Actors are professional story tellers. They are specialists in bringing life to a bare stage. Their skill in creating theatre can also teach us about communication, because speaking in public is also a performance.

Enter the theatre as Richard Burton describes for the BBC Lady Diana Spencer's wedding walk at St Paul's Cathedral. Burton did more than rely on his resonant voice and polished timing. He built a bridge to his audience by asking whether they too had felt a sense of nerves in a crowded room when attention was focused on them. But, as the careful wording shows, like all performers, Burton had rehearsed the moment.

Ah, she's managed those steps, God bless her. She's made it. Now she stands getting ready for that long walk down the aisle. Have you, any of you, had to walk through a crowded room with all eyes on you, and you find the joints of your knees won't work and your back goes rigid and your hands clammy. Well, just think, this young lady is going to have to walk down the aisle with the eyes of five hundred million people watching her. It will take her about three and a half minutes. Go, lovely rose, how sweet and fair she seems to be.

Once a speaker has decided what to say—delivery of the message becomes paramount. Actors learn the power of pausing when delivering lines. Sir Ralph Richardson said that 'pausing is simply everything'. Another person remarked that to err is human, to pause is divine. One actor, turned president, Ronald Reagan, played on his fine sense of theatrical timing at his every public performance.

RONALD REAGAN

Ronald Reagan was asked when he became governor of California, 'What kind of governor will you be?'. He answered, 'I don't know. I've never played a governor.'

Ronald Reagan was the first professional actor in the White House, though most politicians have to be, at the very least, good amateur actors. His election appalled many people who saw his success as the ultimate Hollywood trivialisation. Yet Ronald Reagan was far more than an actor. He earned the tag 'great communicator'. Ronald Reagan had no greater political foe than Senator Edward Kennedy, the standard-bearer of American liberalism. But even Kennedy conceded, in a speech at Yale university, that he admired Ronald Reagan 'because he stood for a set of ideas … he had something to communicate'.

Ronald Reagan's success seemed particularly puzzling to many people living outside America whose image of him was formed by the thirty-second news grabs on television. It was easy to mistake Reagan as merely a ham. But his ideas added substance to the consummate performer. An important element in understanding the Reagan phenomenon is that Americans did not embrace all his ideas. Opinion polls indicated that Americans distinguished between liking the man and not liking many of his views. But having ideas, however unpopular, was a necessary part of the perception that he could be a leader. It didn't matter much about the content of the ideas. In Australia, Joh Bjelke Petersen, another man of minority views, succeeded for much the same reason. An Australian journalist with many decades experience in the United States, Ray Kerrison, says that Reagan's personable style was particularly appealing to the American 'battler'. The American working man loved Ronald Reagan. Of course, this was great for the Republican Party because it meant stealing Democrat votes.

Perhaps Ronald Reagan's finest moment came at a time of national tragedy, on Tuesday, 28 January 1986, the day of the Challenger disaster. The world listened as NASA announced the tragedy:

> This is Mission Control, Houston at 11.48 a.m. Central Standard Time. Recovery teams are searching the impact area off the coast of launch pad 39B where earlier this morning on ascent we had an incident approximately one minute after ascent—an apparent explosion. The search and rescue teams were delayed from getting into the area because debris continued to fall from very high altitudes for as long as an hour after ascent.

On 'AM', the ABC's Jim Middleton took up the story:

> The president had been preparing for his annual state of the union address to congress, normally a triumphant event, when he was passed news of the accident. Like millions of other Americans he quickly turned to a nearby television set to watch replays of the accident. Mr Speakes said Mr Reagan stood in stunned silence as he watched the television.

This was to have been the twenty-fifth space shuttle mission. What was to have made it unique was the presence on board, for the first time, of somebody completely outside the space program, the twenty-seven year old school teacher, Christa McAuliffe. Mrs McAuliffe, the mother of two, couldn't contain her joy at the White House last year when it was announced that she had been selected as the first ordinary American to take part in space flights. 'It's not often that a teacher is at a loss for words,' she said. 'I know that my students wouldn't think so. I've made nine wonderful friends over the past two weeks. And when that shuttle goes there might be one body, but there's going to be ten souls that I'm taking with me.'

After the disaster President Reagan had this to say:

Ladies and gentlemen, I'd planned to speak to you tonight on the state of the union. But the events of earlier today have led me to change those plans. Today is a day for mourning and remembering. Nancy and I are pained to the core by the tragedy of the shuttle Challenger. We share this pain with all of the people of our country. This is truly a national loss. Nineteen years ago, almost to the day, we lost three astronauts in a terrible accident on the ground. But we've never lost an astronaut in flight. We've never had a tragedy like this. And perhaps we've forgotten the courage it took for the crew of the shuttle. But they, the Challenger seven, were aware of the dangers, overcame them, and did their jobs brilliantly. We mourn seven heroes—Michael Smith, Dick Scobee, Judith Resnik, Ronald McNair, Ellison Onizuka, Gregory Jarvis and Christa McAuliffe. We mourn their loss as a nation together. To the families of the seven: we cannot bear, as you do, the full impact of this tragedy. But we feel the loss, and we're thinking about you so very much. Your loved ones were daring and brave and they had that special grace, that special spirit which said 'give me a challenge and I will meet it with joy'. They had a hunger to explore the universe and discover its truths. They wished to serve and they did. They served all of us. We've grown used to wonders in this century. It's hard to dazzle us. But for twenty-five years the United States space program has been doing just that. We've grown used to the idea of space, and perhaps we forget that we've only just begun. We're still pioneers. They, the members of the Challenger crew were pioneers. There's a coincidence today. On this day, three hundred and ninety years ago, the great explorer Sir Francis Drake died aboard ship off the coast of Panama. In his lifetime the great frontiers were the oceans and an historian later said, he lived by the sea, died on it and was buried in it. Well today, we can say of the Challenger crew, their dedication was like Drake's, complete. The crew of the space shuttle Challenger honoured us for the manner in which they lived their lives. We will never forget them nor the last time we saw them, this morning, as they prepared for their journey and waved goodbye, and slipped the surly bonds of earth to touch the face of God. Thank you.

The Challenger address was the work of one of Ronald Reagan's speechwriters, Peggy Noonan. The speech was partly written from the notes of a conversation with Ronald Reagan when the Challenger news broke.

Peggy Noonan has written a book about her experiences as the president's speechwriter. It's called *What I Saw at the Revolution*. She spoke to Scott Simon from American Public Radio.

NOONAN: When you work with a president on a speech and he gives that speech, those are his words. If they are words that make a promise, the American people will hold him to that promise, as in 'read my lips'.

SIMON: You write about getting a speech through a group of people you call the mice in the White House and the State Department. What is that process like?

NOONAN: Well, it's a very tough process for a writer. In modern White Houses, speechwriters tend to be, in my opinion, a little too far removed from the president they are working for. An important speech would go out to fifty, a hundred, sometimes more people, all of whom had the right, as persons of authority, to delete sentences, to add sentences, to drop whole pages and paragraphs, to sometimes add new points of view. And, as the speechwriter, I was charged with gathering all these comments and putting them sometimes in a whole new speech which was sometimes quite impossible.

SIMON: You once circulated a memo in the White House showing what the staffing process would do to the Gettysburg address. What I had in mind is if you would read the words of Lincoln and maybe for theatrical effect I would read the words of the staffers which you scrawl in:

(Noonan and Simon reading a script.)

NOONAN: 'Four score and seven years ago ...'

SIMON: 'Now, stop right there. *Eighty-seven years ago*, or maybe *long ago*. We'll figure that out later. Go ahead.'

NOONAN: '... our fathers...'

SIMON: 'Lets add, *and mothers*.'

NOONAN: '... brought forth upon this continent ...'

SIMON: 'I think *created* here would probably be clearer.'

NOONAN: 'a new nation conceived in liberty ...'

SIMON: 'Can't do that. Too much sexual imagery. Sounds like you're talking about teen pregnancy or something.'

NOONAN: '... and dedicated to the proposition ...'

SIMON: 'No, *idea*. I think *idea* is a more direct word. Go ahead please.'

NOONAN: 'that all men ...'

SIMON: '*and women*'

NOONAN: '… are created equal.'

SIMON: '*Equally*, I think is grammatically correct. Go ahead please.'

NOONAN: 'Now we are engaged …'

SIMON: '*Fighting*. Fighting I think is what you mean there.'

NOONAN: '… in a great civil war …'

SIMON: 'No, no, no, no. *Great*? What's so great about it? It's a civil war. Go ahead please.'

NOONAN: '… testing whether that nation …'

SIMON: 'Mmm. No, what nation do you mean? Go ahead.'

NOONAN: '… or any nation, so conceived …'

SIMON: 'There's that word again. Have to drop it.'

NOONAN: '… and so dedicated can long endure.'

SIMON: What was the reception when you circulated this?

NOONAN: I just sent it out to my friends. They laughed, they yukked it up, ha, ha. Peggy is acting up again.

SIMON: Could we count on both hands the number of times you met with President Reagan?

NOONAN: Maybe three hands, I guess, in all. And that included five or six times when I was working with him on his farewell address. That was the most I ever got to see of him or know him.

SIMON: Is that part of the problem with speechwriting, that there is so little premium placed on the president actually contributing his or her own words?

NOONAN: You know, Lincoln probably spoke once a week. Modern presidents speak five, six or seven times a day frequently. So they can't sit down and write these things. That's why speechwriters exist. Cal Coolidge hired the first one.

Across the Atlantic, Britain's longest serving prime minister of this century, Margaret Thatcher, envied the communication powers of Ronald Reagan. Hugo Young, the author of the Thatcher biography, *One of Us*, had this to say about Margaret Thatcher's view of Ronald Reagan as a communicator:

She looks at Reagan who was, one has to remember, by origin an actor, who had vast experience as a communicator of that kind on film and also on radio and who made, when he was president, on radio, a tremendous success of his weekly broadcasts in which he spoke with what appeared to be genuine sincerity to the people at large. Now I know that Margaret Thatcher looked at Reagan as a great communicator. People used to ask how could it be that she admired him so much because he was clearly so stupid and she was clearly so clever; he was so slow, she was so quick; he was so dull, she was so sharp. And the answer I always found when inquiring about it was that for all her awareness of his weaknesses and his considerable lack of intellect compared with hers, she recognised completely someone who could communicate, who had this fantastic gift of drawing in the audience and appearing to sincerely convey a message.

I asked Christine Maher what the key to Reagan's success was. Maher replied:

He had the gift of simplicity. He was criticised by what I will term the *intellectuals* who said it's too simplistic, but he understood that good communication depends on having one idea and expressing it in a way which is easily understood—did they hear, did they understand, and did you move them to think or take the actions that you wanted to?

Hugh Mackay had this to say about Ronald Reagan as a communicator:

Reagan I believe fulfilled the American people's desire for a fully regal figure, for a monarchy in a sense. He was the consummate presidential-style person. I don't mean by that that he was empty, that he was a puppet. What I do mean is that he played the part exactly as the American people want their presidents to play that part. And it's significant that he often said things that were non sequiturs or just plain wrong or rather incoherent, but like our own prime minister, in a way, the words he said were not the crucial thing. It was the manner in which they were said that was so impressive to his audience.

Here is more from Scott Simon's interview with Reagan's speechwriter, and author, Peggy Noonan:

NOONAN: You cannot take a dull stone of a man and turn him into something that he is not. I frequently get asked: 'Gee, isn't there something potentially dangerous; could a clever speechwriter and a clever media handler get this hollow vessel of a candidate and fill him up and could he win?' And I honestly think, yeah, he could win just about as far as Iowa. I mean we see them so much, we see right through them. I do think ultimately you can judge the personality and the character of the people and you can't pull off a grand fraud.

SIMON: You realise what you're describing is to some people the story of the presidency of Ronald Reagan?

NOONAN: That's because they're confused. Look, Ronald Reagan was in politics for serious political reasons. He wanted to change America, to pick it up, shake it a little bit and change where it was. He wanted to change our minds. He wasn't there for some sort of vague, amorphous, wistful desire to be a leader in a picture.

SIMON: You write in the book that the president literally never feels the cold.

NOONAN: M-m. Isn't that funny? Presidents stay hermetically sealed in an environment. There's a sense in the men around the White House: 'don't chill the franchise, don't let him get a cold'. There's also a sense that the president should never have nothing to do. You know how sometimes you go to the car in the driveway and you notice there's a little snow on the windshield and you knock it off and you look at your hand for a second, maybe you daydream for a minute. Presidents are never allowed to stand and daydream. Presidents are always being directed 'over here sir; you can sit here now; sir, it's cold, why don't we go inside, why don't we wait in the limo?'.

SIMON: How intelligent is it to be left with almost a sense of sorrow for Ronald Reagan?

NOONAN: M-m. I still don't know if I'm right about this but I have the sense that he was lonely. You know, people who put up walls and don't let other people in, they may feel safe but I cannot help but think they also feel somewhat estranged and alone. I convince myself of this and then I'll see him, every few months, waving across a room and I'll get a look at him up close and actually he does appear to be a happy man, who is happy with life and trusts it. So I can never quite get it figured out what exactly I think. He is for me, ultimately, a huge paradox.

Peggy Noonan's own story about how presidents are never allowed to daydream is a fine example of a well-told story which gets a point across.

For a final word on Ronald Reagan and his style, I spoke to Stephen Mills—long-serving speechwriter to Bob Hawke.

MILLS: I think if Hawke and Australian politicians generally started issuing forth with that kind of poetry, with the deep blue sky kind of rhetoric that the Americans get away with, that Reagan excelled in, I think that they would be looked at as soft in the head.

We will analyse the one time powerful communications skills of former Prime Minister Bob Hawke in Part Four.

HUMOUR

Telling a story with humour—seeing the absurd in the world and ourselves—is the most infectious communication technique. It bonds the speaker to the audience through the sharing of laughter. I consulted Hugh Mackay on the subject:

When people start laughing they are giving an emotional response almost in spite of themselves. They are being caught up in the message because they're laughing. So, humour is a great thing to use for unlocking the emotions and it's why good communicators often begin with amusing things to get people into the mood of relaxation. Shakespeare understood this very well. Make sure that every now and then people are laughing. Partly it's good deep-breathing exercise to freshen them up for a more serious point which is going to follow but also it just gets them onside.

But, of course, there are moments when humour must be absolutely avoided in order to emphasise the seriousness of what we're about.

I put the following question to Hugh Mackay: 'If people feel they aren't very funny themselves but want to make people laugh, can they do that?'

They can only do it by telling structured jokes which is very dangerous. I mean if you're not an amusing person I don't think you can learn to be but you can, of course, tell little stories which are funny. And that is a good way to establish rapport with your audience if it doesn't come naturally.

Sometimes what is funny is nothing more than an accurate reflection of what people are thinking and especially what they are saying in their own lives. David Williamson's plays are excruciatingly funny because they remind people of an absurdity in themselves or of an unresolved conflict. Being given permission to laugh is just a great relief.

SUMMARY

When you tell stories rather than talk abstractly people remember what you say. The simpler the story, the clearer the point you make. It's why people often remember jokes. They're among the simplest stories.

The crucial point about the power of stories is that the right story can make the profound simple, not simplistic. You don't need to be highly intelligent or articulate to tell good stories and be a great communicator. In fact, people who think and talk in complexities start with a disadvantage. They won't get their message across. Academic training is particularly destructive of lucid communication. Few academics dare to express themselves simply for fear of being ridiculed as simple-minded by their colleagues. Many academics, particularly in the social sciences, dismiss a well-told story as mere anecdote. Academic rigour should never be confused with effective communication.

Great communicators do more than get their point across. They get people to act. In the next section we see how community and business leaders get people moving.

WHAT YOU CAN DO

Set out to develop stories which illustrate the points you want to make in your presentations. They can, of course, be told more than once. Some years ago, when I was involved in the conservation campaign for Tasmania's Franklin River, I was having a conversation with Don Chipp, the leader of the Australian Democrats. He asked me why Tasmanians shouldn't be allowed to work out the fate of the Franklin by themselves. I replied that it would be like leaving the fate of the Great Barrier Reef to the people of a few towns in Queensland—Townsville and Gladstone. Chipp was a bowerbird for stories. I heard him repeat that answer time and again. A communicator is always on the look out for the right way of expressing something, the right story.

Stories need rehearsal. They can always be expressed more simply. The timing can always be better. The best stories are personal stories we feel strongly about. Search your own experiences. Our own stories are unique. As eyewitnesses, we can bring them alive.

PART FOUR

THE CALL TO ACTION
'Ask what you can do for your country'

'And so my fellow Americans, ask not what your country can do for you. Ask what you can do for your country.' These are the words with which President John F Kennedy, at his inauguration, issued a classic call to action. In Part Four we analyse the role of calling people to action—of getting a response to what we say. We'll also discuss how to succeed in business communication, and ponder what happened to Bob Hawke's once great gift for getting his message across.

Once a communicator has discovered the secrets of talking in powerful language and metaphor, of talking with emotion, of talking in stories and parables, the audience is ready to act. But people must be called to action. Hugh Mackay of Mackay Research in Sydney had this to say:

> People are finally only captured by a message, finally will only give themselves to a message when it's clear to them how they can translate that message into some action in their personal lives. Without the feeling that I'm committed to action in my own behaviour, communication is just ghostly, just a shadowy little experience. It needs to be tied to reality.

At times of great national crisis—in war—leaders don't simply assume that people will act. They call them to action. They call them to arms. Recall Winston Churchill:

We shall fight on the beaches. We shall fight on the landing grounds. We shall fight in the fields and in the streets. We shall fight in the hills. We shall never surrender.

In Australia, Robert Menzies, as wartime prime minister, made this declaration in the Sydney Town Hall on 26 May 1941, a few months before his government fell from office.

We are not to escape our responsibility for this moment by pointing either to the past or to the future. This is the present. We are the actors in the present. We have a powerful foe to fight and we can win only if we are united in function, united in action, as I know we are in spirit and belief.

After Menzies resigned, John Curtin, the new prime minister also spoke at the Sydney Town Hall, on the steps outside, as he opened the Liberty Loan on 17 February 1942. He, too, called the nation to action:

This is the call I make unto you, for war is a bloody thing, war is a killing thing. There is need for vigilance. Everywhere there is the requirement of industry. Everywhere there is the obligation of order. Everywhere there is demanded of us a degree of cooperative citizenship such as never in our history have we yet attained. And we can do these things my fellow citizens for there's nothing that any other race can do upon this earth that we Australians are not capable of doing.

John F Kennedy's call to action at his inauguration in 1961 at the height of the Cold War used both the rhetoric of war and peace.

Now the trumpet summons us again, not as a call to bear arms, though arms we need. Not as a call to battle, though in battle we are. But a call to bear the burden of a long twilight struggle, year in and year out, rejoicing in hope, patient in tribulation, a struggle against the common enemies of man: tyranny, poverty, disease and war itself. Will you join in that historic effort?

The energy, the faith, the devotion which we bring to this endeavour will light our country and all who serve it and the glow from that fire can truly light the world. And so, my fellow Americans, ask not what your country can do for you. Ask what you can do for your country. My fellow citizens of the world, ask not what America will do for you but what together we can do for the freedom of man.

In 1972, at the Australian Labor Party's campaign launch, Gough Whitlam cleverly used repetition as a means of reinforcing his call for action to change the government:

Men and women of Australia. The decision we will make for

our country on 2 December is a choice between the past and the future; between the habits and fears of the past and the demands and opportunities of the future. There are moments in history when the whole fate and future of nations can be decided by a single decision. For Australia, this is such a time. It's time for a new team, a new program, a new drive for equality of opportunity. It's time to create new opportunities for Australians, time for a new vision of what we can achieve in this generation for our nation and for the region in which we live. It's time for a new government.

In another example, the Aboriginal rock singer Monica Morgan issued a passionate call for action to black and white Australians:

I'm putting it out there to all the non-Aboriginal people. You can't sit there and expect the Australian government to be the ones to give recognition of our existence. You can't sit by. And us Koori people—we can't wait always for our organisations to be the ones to lead the way for us. We all gather together and we all make our voice strong. Because in the end, it's our children that we have to make our future for. And there can be no justice until there's recognition of where we come from. And we come from this land and we've got to write that history.

In politics, calls to action often ask people to work together. The following excerpts are from Britain's Neil Kinnock in a keynote address to a trade union congress; and from President Bush at his inauguration (in a speech written with the assistance of Peggy Noonan):

We're going to have to work our way out of this mess and we're going to have to work our way out of this mess together. There is not other practical way for this country. (Neil Kinnock)

America is never wholly herself unless she is engaged in high moral principle. We as a people have such a purpose today. It is to make kinder the face of the nation and gentler the face of the world. My friends, we have work to do. (George Bush)

Great communicators call people to action. And the more specific the call, the more likely it is to be heeded. People are empowered through action. It is therefore vital that the call to action be a positive statement which will affirm people's desire to have control over their lives.

Although a call to action may come at the end of a speech or presentation, it ought to be thought about first during your preparation. After all, calling people to action is the point of most communication.

COMMUNICATION
IN BUSINESS

A surprising number of business leaders don't understand how to get their message across. Their communication skills are often far inferior to their general professional skills. To put it in business language, they can't sell a message.

Christine Maher of Celebrity Speakers is a consultant to business on communication:

> The American Management Association published the results of a survey some years ago. They surveyed two hundred chief executives from small, medium and large-size companies over a period of two years and they asked them to pick between different components of a speech. And the figures are quite surprising. Who was speaking and why they should listen to them was quite important and they rated that as having a value of forty per cent. What was said was also important but that rated only seven per cent. The major difference was how it was said.

I asked communications consultant Dr Peter Kenny to assess some well-known business communicators:

THOMPSON: Dick Smith, what would you say about him?

KENNY: Yes, he's a good communicator. Face to face you can't get a word in edgewise. But when he gets on screen, his over-the-top style carries him, because it gets him to the cliff edge. He's a persistently irritating person, especially face to face, and even on the TV he's persistently irritating and that works for him. He keeps your attention.

THOMPSON: Is Bob Ansett a good communicator?

KENNY: He's not bad, not bad, a bit cold. His delivery is fairly cold, don't you think?

It's hard to think of good business communicators. They don't stick out. They're too stitched up, they're careful, they complete their sentences, they write everything down neat and tidy, they make lists of things, agendas for meetings, they plan things and all of that is contrary to communication. The more neat and tidy you are the worse your communication gets.

A lot of my clients won't go to the cliff edge. They do wimpy advertising. They won't address their boards and meetings honestly and openly. They write stuff down which is censored and tidied up before they convey it to their subordinates, and of course their subordinates know that. Sitting there in the hall, they're thinking—here's a stitched up, tidied up quarterly report for our consumption which doesn't tell us the truth about what's happening in this company.

I asked Christine Maher of Celebrity Speakers: 'Are business people good communicators?'.

MAHER: Generally not. They operate on the intellectual level. I was once asked by a business magazine to give a list of the ten worst business communicators in Australia and I declined on the basis that it would unfairly discriminate against all the rest.

Business speakers generally have a problem with their speeches. They are badly written, they are over-complicated. They read them, they ignore the audience, there is absolutely no energy in the presentation and they are grim. And if you ever walk into a business conference and you see these serious-faced, stony-faced people standing up, reading papers that the audience is reading along with them, then you know that there is something seriously wrong with the system.

Truth works in communication. Sincerity always works in communication—a more casual, relaxed, direct style of speaking. And part of the reason why we like some speakers and don't like others or don't trust them is because we suspect what they are saying doesn't quite gel with what they are thinking.

Tom Peters is the author of the world's number-one-selling business book, *In Search of Excellence*. He understands the need for passion in business communication. Business leaders pay fortunes to hear his brand of passion. A Tom Peters seminar keeps people awake because of its energy. His mobility about the seminar room ensures that his presence fills each corner. The atmosphere is charged by a combination of evangelical zeal and more serious points of analysis.

Tom Peters also wrote the world's second most successful business book, *A Passion for Excellence*, with Nancy Austin. She also tours the world communicating about business strategy. A Nancy Austin seminar has much in common with the Tom Peters' style. She is cooler in her presentation but she works to be inspirational. She always illustrates her concepts with detailed and powerful anecdotes. Nancy Austin talks simply, in stories, such as this one she told to me about the troubles faced by Bob Ansett:

He was delightfully close to his customers from what I have read about him and I think he did get half of it right. The half he had right was the passionate devotion to customers and customer service. The half of it he apparently missed is the need to have a system, that is, you've got to be organised. I heard a story that he hopped over the counter one day at Budget and helped all these customers when he saw there was a long line. He helped eight customers but he only remembered to collect money from three.

'NARROWCASTING'

In this book, we have focused on broadcasting or how to get a message across to large numbers of people. But leaders need to 'narrowcast' too. Narrowcasting is getting a message across to people in small groups or even one at a time. Narrowcasters get the chance to listen as well as talk. It's time-consuming but it gets results.

Two distinguished business leaders—James Strong, the former head of Australian Airlines, and Ivan Deveson, the former chief of Nissan Australia—are specialists in narrowcasting.

The key role that management adds is to provide some vision, to say we might be here now but in a few years we can be there. Some people will say: that's crazy, we can't achieve that. So what you do then is to break it up into a whole series of practical little steps for each area of the business and go out and sell that to them. And by that process you begin to get people to think differently, to act differently. The strategy was based on me personally selling that to them. And every year I've been in the airline I've gone around and tried to talk to every staff member in direct talks, which is very time-consuming but very rewarding. (James Strong)

I need to be walking about at least fifty per cent of my time. I'm walking about right now talking to you. I'm away from my desk, I'm away from the board room. And walking about means not only walking the factory assembly lines or the machine shops but face to face with customers, dealers, suppliers, government officials, people in the marketplace. Getting the feel for business, getting the feel from employees. Listening, talking and most of all, feeling the atmosphere of what's going right and what's going wrong. (Ivan Deveson)

A worker at Nissan had this assessment of Ivan Deveson: 'I think everybody knows Ivan Deveson. He talks to the people. He asks the people have they got any problems, how do they feel working with Nissan'.

BOB HAWKE

In *The Secrets of the Great Communicators* I have stressed that the techniques of communication can be learned. They can also be forgotten. The story of Bob Hawke's failing communication skills is a cautionary lesson to people who obtain power and influence, and then duck for cover. It can leave their communication vapid.

Hugh Mackay had these comments when I spoke to him about Bob Hawke in the latter days of his government:

MACKAY: Bob Hawke is a good communicator when he does what the Australian people really want him to do, which is act like one of them. The reason why so much emotional investment was made in Hawke was that he portrayed himself, and people responded favourably to it, as a man of the people. When he misses out is when he starts appearing aristocratic and arrogant and aloof.

THOMPSON: Can you be prime minister without appearing aristocratic and aloof?

MACKAY: Yes, I think you can and I think he was successfully doing that during his first term. I think that position has been eroded but it is what the people loved him for, and it's the remnants of that that they still love him for.

Christine Maher offered the following observations:

MAHER: In the early days Bob Hawke was such a good communicator because he was obviously very involved himself in whatever he was saying. He's pulled back from that now, I suspect on the advice of his minders, and so he's not nearly as good.

THOMPSON: Is Bob Hawke boring now?

MAHER: Yes. Boring because he has let the fire and the passion go out of what he's saying. I think he's concentrating on being a statesman and trying to say the right thing. And once you do that you lose the ability to contact people.

THOMPSON: What would you say to Bob Hawke to correct that problem.

MAHER: Oh, I would love to have half a day with him and

get him back to where he was before. I would tell him that he should certainly think carefully about what he is going to say, but I would help him to rediscover, to feel what it is that he's saying.

Bob Hawke certainly used to feel what he said. This is the old Hawke, the pre-prime ministerial Hawke: 'You see, I am a socialist ...'. On another occasion:

It's about time that the people of Australia understood the pernicious hypocrisy of your Murdochs and Packers who talk about the freedom of the press. When they talk about the freedom of the press they have a special definition. It's the freedom to push their own personal interests. While they think they can treat the Australian electorate as a pack of unintelligent fools who can be led like sheep, they and Mr Fraser should understand that Mr Fraser might be able to herd his sheep on his eight thousand acre property at Nareen in the western districts but the Australian electors are not like sheep on his Nareen property. They will not be herded by the lies and mendacity of these people.

Now, how far do you reduce real wages? Do we reduce real wages by fifty per cent? Is that going to restore employment? Who's going to buy the goods? Are we going to have an invasion from Mars and a sudden consumer demand coming from extra-terrestrial sources? Or do we cut them by three-quarters? Or why should we pay workers anything? And then everything would be beautiful. Employers wouldn't have any costs and we would be competitive, but who would buy the goods? Now this is not playing funny chaps with argument. It's getting right down to the guts of what they're about.

The problem with the old Hawke was that his communication was far too direct for the comfort of many Australians. His minders feared that Hawke the great communicator would not succeed as prime minister. So they worked to ensure that Bob Hawke, PM, remained largely incident-free—free of incidents like the interview with Richard Carleton on the night he became Labor leader in 1983.

CARLETON: Mr Hawke, could I ask you whether you were feeling a little embarrassed tonight at the blood that's on your hands?
HAWKE: You're not improving are you, I thought you'd make a better start to the year than that. It's a ridiculous question and you know it's ridiculous. I have no blood on my hands.
CARLETON: Can you expect people to believe that you didn't

know that that meeting was to take place?

HAWKE: I can expect people to believe that you are a damned impertinence.

In more recent times, the old Bob Hawke has occasionally resurfaced. He told a pensioner he was a 'silly old bugger'. He told a bishop that his postcard campaign against politicians' attitudes to child poverty was 'a bloody disgrace'. And on the first full day of campaigning for the 1990 election, he lost his patience at being crowded by media microphones on a lectern: 'Look, just get that bloody thing out of there and let me show you what I want and you get around it, eh'.

Political research showed that Bob Hawke's outbursts were an electoral liability. A new Hawke had to be engineered. What has emerged, in often painful syntax, reveals the dangers of manufacturing an unnatural communication style:

It was absolutely implicit in what I said then what I am making explicit now. Perhaps, I concede this, perhaps it would have been more sensible in the light of, you know, how it's developed, it may have been more sensible if I had spelled out in explicit terms what was implicit. But I think you can see that what I have said subsequently is an explicit statement of what was implicit. And I have no objections that people have wanted me, and the media for instance have been involved, in getting that explicit statement.

Hawke's performances were not all painful syntax. Bob Hawke could still be a great communicator. Stephen Mills was the Prime Minister's speechwriter from 1986 to 1991. In his Parliament House office he spoke to me about his job:

I'm only writing the text. It is Bob Hawke who has to get up and deliver them. And Bob Hawke does that effectively, obviously when he has a text that he is comfortable with. But that's not the end of the story. He establishes his own rapport with an audience. And you can almost see this happening in a physical sense. Hawke has the capacity to understand the components of an audience, to put them at ease. He is a popular politician for a very good reason, that people enjoy being in his company.

Be it on a one-to-one basis, or a one-to-one thousand basis, they all feel as though they are getting something personal from Bob Hawke. And he can, with or without a text, be the passionate Hawke, the articulate Hawke, the policy activist Hawke.

There are times when he's clear and times when he's less clear.

I think critics are wrong when they say he is boring because I don't think any fair judgment of him in a crowd would say that it's a boring presentation. It's often, I find, full of electricity and fire.

CONCLUSION

What have we learned? What are the secrets of the great communicators?

Overwhelmingly the thing a great communicator must have is an understanding of the mind and the mood of the audience with whom he or she wants to communicate. There are no other rules. (Hugh Mackay)

They've got to go down into the audience. They've got to touch the audience, shake hands with people, speak to them. They've got to gather the audience as close to them as they can and not remain distant. Ask the audience to come to you. They will start to say: 'Will you tell us about this? Will you tell us about that?' Now you've got a two way communication going instead of one way. (Peter Kenny)

We don't make decisions based on facts. We don't make decisions logically, generally. Most decisions are based on emotion. We need and we look for facts to justify those decisions. (Christine Maher)

Tell them to forget about data. Data is shackles. Data is history, gone, in one end, out the other. Why talk about past history? Direct yourself at the future, at what can happen, at what should happen now. (Peter Kenny)

I once saw a man stand up at a conference and ask the speaker if he was going to read his paper. The speaker was slightly flustered and said, 'Yes I am'. And the man said, 'Thank you very much, in that case please post it to me because I can read it faster and better than you can'. (Christine Maher)

Boredom is the most destructive, aggressive, damaging thing you can do to people. Speakers must have what they want to say so deeply ingrained in their person that they can stand up and simply say it spontaneously as they would to their family or as they would to their children.

They must know their topic. It's an insult for someone to read out a speech to you. It means they don't know enough about it or aren't comfortable enough to speak to you naturally about it as they ought to. (Peter Kenny)

You don't have to be articulate. You don't have to be intelligent. You don't have to be literate. What you have to be is sensitive. (Hugh Mackay)

And we all know people who are not the best and brightest minds in an organisation but who have the ability to sell a message and they always attract more attention. It's the emotional involvement of a person with what they are saying. (Christine Maher)

The way you get credibility is by dropping your pants and being completely human and honest. (Peter Kenny)

A speech is like a picture. You use broad strokes to sketch in. If there is a lot of detail we need to see it in written form, so you paint the broad picture and then give details in a printed handout. (Christine Maher)

It's the role of the speech to put all the jigsaw pieces down and to show the picture, the coherent picture. (Stephen Mills)

Listening is ninety-five per cent of the skill of communication. I mean understanding what's in the mind of your audience already; getting to know them so that you can express what you want to say in a way that they can respond to. So you know they can respond before you speak. (Hugh Mackay)

Be unashamedly showbiz and accept that. Anyone in theatre or a singer or a concert performer will tell you that's when it works best. Kiri Te Kanawa will say that her best performances were when she went out there, prepared, but then pushed herself beyond her limit, beyond the limit of her controllable voice and took the full risk and got the standing ovation. (Peter Kenny)

You don't need to be a Churchill, Kennedy, Martin Luther King, Reagan or Hawke to be a great communicator. Ernie Guest stormed the beach at Gallipolli with the ANZACS. Now in his nineties, Ernie Guest has all the talents of a great communicator. He gave this interview to 'AM''s Sarah Armstrong on the eve of his return to Gallipolli on the seventy-fifth anniversary of the landing:

GUEST: I am not an emotional man. I'm a realist and I'll go there and my mind will go back to where we lost some of our best mates. I'll go and have a look at their graves and then I can come home.

ARMSTRONG: How do you think Gallipolli will have changed in the time since you've been there?

GUEST: Well, you won't be looking up in the bushes to see where the sniper is having a go at you.

ARMSTRONG: How do you feel about meeting Turkish people when you're there?

GUEST: They're fine people, the best snipers in the world. I've got no enmity against the Turk whatsoever. Could I tell you a little story? We in Australia were all volunteers. Now what happened about the Turk? He was conscripted. And ninety-nine per cent of those Turks never had a spare shilling. What have I got against him? They were dirty and lousy, same as I was, and they never had anything. No, I'd be pleased to shake the Turk's hand and say, well, he's a gentleman too, as I'd hope to be.

WHAT YOU CAN DO

Work out a call to action as the first step in preparing your presentation. Be clear about what you want people to do. The call to action is usually presented at the end of the presentation.

- Research your audience. Then you'll know what bridges to build to connect with them.
- Do not read speeches. They bore people. Prepare notes but remember that the best notes are single, prompt words.
- Do not overload speeches with facts. Detailed facts should be presented in written handouts. Overheads and illustrations must also be absolutely simple or you will distract the audience's attention away from you.
- Be like Kiri Te Kanawa and get the standing ovation. Take risks by going to the cliff edge, by going beyond your imagined limits.

EPILOGUE

How do the secrets of the great communicators relate to us ordinary mortals? Is there anything to learn from these people, many of whose lives were bound up with history-making events? For us, addressing our business colleagues and associates or speaking to a local community group may be a far less lofty enterprise than when Churchill spoke to a wartime audience. However, we can vastly improve our own communication power by emulating the techniques of the great communicators.

Managing is a communication process. We should pay as much attention to developing our communication skills as we pay to the understanding of marketing, strategy, or reading the bottom line. The most common error made by executives is to confuse communication with the transfer of information. I have watched as many high-powered managers crowd their public presentations with technical mumbo jumbo and seem determined to include every known fact on their subject, even in a short address. They seem oblivious when their audience retains little or none of what they are saying.

Great communicators work differently. They identify with their audience and its needs, they understand what their audience is feeling, and they understand what their audience is saying. In turn, the audience identifies with the communicator as a person, it understands the communicator's feelings, and it understands what the communicator is saying. When this interactive process is at work, true communication is taking place. It will be risky for some managers who are used to old-style techniques of control, and who present their ideas in a didactic manner. They tend to be defensive if challenged.

The techniques of the great communicators—their willingness to talk with emotion and to talk in stories and metaphors—may seem alien and uncomfortable at first. If this applies to you, then you should start listening and analysing everyday communication—around home, in business, on radio and television. Consider for yourself what is working and why.

ACKNOWLEDGMENTS

Many people have contributed their ideas and time to this project. Jean Walker was invaluable in assisting me to sift through the great collection in ABC Radio Archives. Jean also listened with a critical ear to the programs as they took shape.

My colleagues at ABC Current Affairs were of great assistance in providing technical and editorial assistance for the radio series. My thanks to Johnny Bwin, Fred Bostan, Martin Leech, Margaret Paap, Paul McKercher, Leonie Highfield, Anne McCaig and Michael Dodd.

Colin Pidd from ABC Radio's 'Managing Matters' supplied material from his program file. Other ABC broadcasters compiled many of the interviews contained in this series but are not mentioned by name. I am indebted to them too.

Janie Lalor of ABC Television was vital to the completion of the accompanying videotape.

Thanks also to Amanda Solomon of ABC Radio Publicity for her assistance in researching the photographic material for inclusion in this book and the video. The support of Robert Gibbs also helped get the project started. Brian McInerny processed the photographic materials.

Peter Steiner and Tara McCarthy were both great sources of advice.

I particularly want to thank those who gave their time to be interviewed—Hugh Mackay of Mackay Research, Dr Peter Kenny, Christine Maher of Celebrity Speakers, Stephen Mills, who was speech writer to Bob Hawke, Jonathan West and Bob Brown.

Thanks to Richard Smart, Stuart Neal, Janine Burdeu, Jean Attwater and Bernadette Neubecker at ABC Enterprises and the team at ABC Legal who supervised and conducted the copyright search—Allison Rowe, Ali Edwards and Michael Chessell.

My partner and wife, Lissa Tarleton, cast a careful eye over the text and suggested many changes.